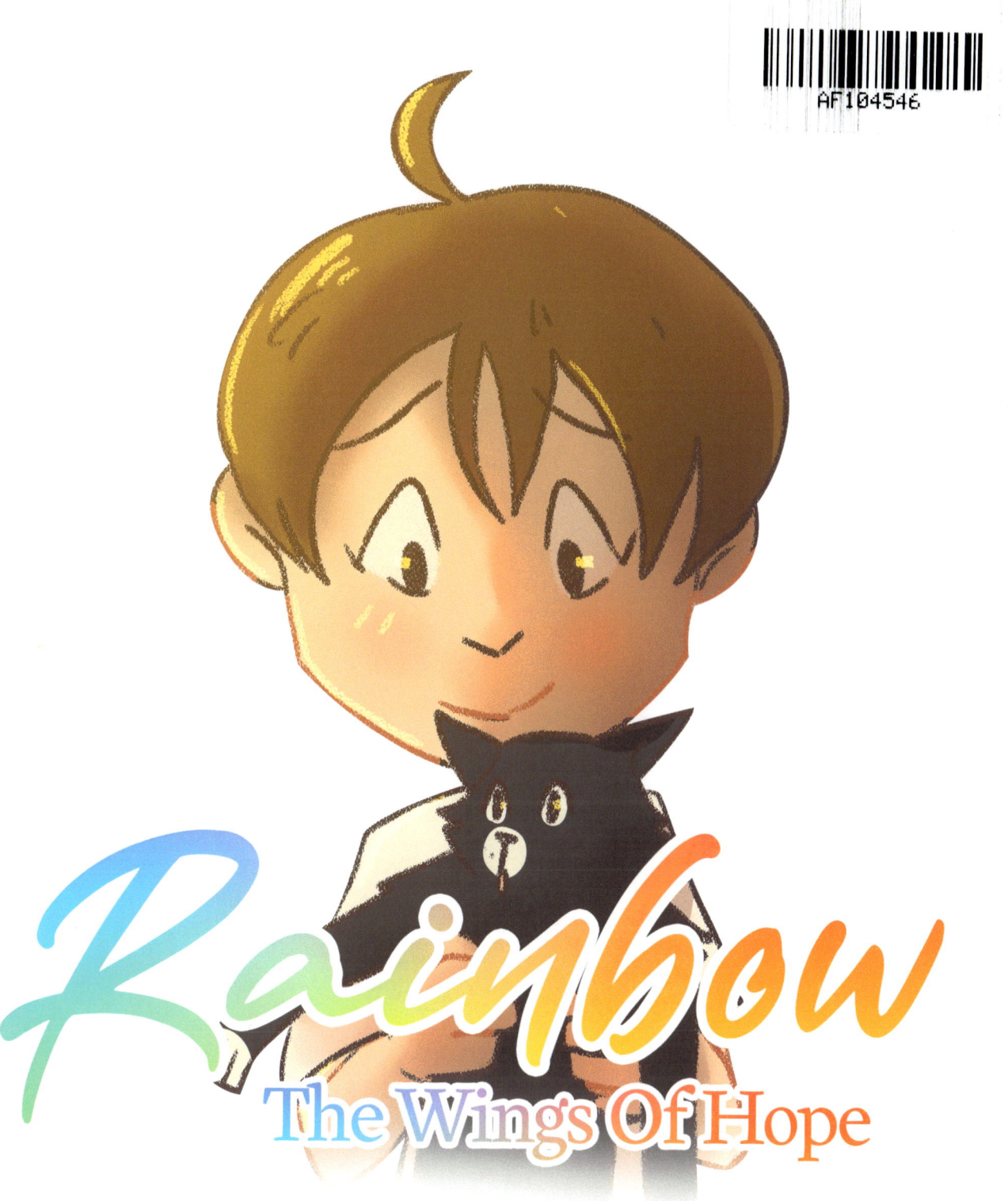

Rainbow
The Wings Of Hope

Written by
Consuelo Isabel Pimentel

Illustrated by
Stefanie St. Denis

Rainbow
Copyright © 2023 by Consuelo Isabel Pimentel

All rights reserved. No part of this publication may be reproduced, distributed, or transmitted in any form or by any means, including photocopying, recording, or other electronic or mechanical methods, without the prior written permission of the author, except in the case of brief quotations embodied in critical reviews and certain other non-commercial uses permitted by copyright law.

Tellwell Talent
www.tellwell.ca

ISBN
978-0-2288-9008-9 (Hardcover)
978-0-2288-9007-2 (Paperback)

To my husband Michael, for giving
me the courage to dream;

to my little boy Orlando, you are
the biggest blessing in our lives;

and to my angel baby Bella,
you will always be loved.

Once upon a time, a little boy named Anthony saw something special in the balcony...

He asked his mom what it was.

Two lovely birds made a nest and laid an egg inside, she said. Very soon, a baby bird will arrive.

Anthony's eyes lit up and he jumped with joy. He drew pictures of everything that happened. He really enjoyed this.

One day, a big pigeon tried to eat the egg. The dad bird flew in to protect the egg.

Anthony would sneak close to see the parents cuddle their egg in the afternoon, and he would whisper: Your baby will be here soon.

When a bird parent came flying in, Anthony's cat hissed at them. Anthony took his cat away so the bird parents would feel safe.

Many days went by, but no baby bird hatched. Mom could see how Anthony had become so attached.

Mom said, Sweetie, before you came, Daddy and I were waiting for a baby, just like the bird parents. We took good care of our baby Bella, but she never hatched. We were very sad, but we always hoped that one day you would come along.

Sometimes babies are not born; we don't understand why. It was nobody's fault. Would you like to say goodbye? Mom asked.

But I was excited to meet Dottie, Anthony said. I named her Dottie because of the dark dots on her shell.

Anthony and his parents went on a vacation to try and cheer him up. Anthony prayed that wherever Dottie was, she would know that they still loved her so much.

Dad made a paper lantern. He helped Anthony write a letter that said: Sending love up above.

When they returned home, Anthony went to grab his scooter. Then he heard a tiny squeak that couldn't be any cuter.

His heart was racing. He looked around, and this time there were three birds to count!

Anthony called his parents. They were all happy to finally see a baby bird with her family.

What do you want to call the baby? Mom asked.

I will name her Rainbow, because after a rain... comes sunshine, said Anthony.

The End

www.ingramcontent.com/pod-product-compliance
Lightning Source LLC
LaVergne TN
LVHW071655060526
838200LV00029B/465